Today I'll work in the garden.

But where are my work gloves? I put them in a safe place...Was it under the newspaper?

I'll just put on my bow tie and think. Aha! My gloves are behind this pillow!

I'll just slip on my socks, then I'll look under the bed!

I'll just put on my hat and...
Oh! I remember!

I put something under
my yellow raincoat!

I'll just hop into my shoes
and...I've got it! I'll
look under the piano lid!

I'll put on my scarf
and...what is that bump?
My gloves must be under
that rug!

I'll throw on my jacket,
but I need my gloves!
Maybe they're outside.
I'll look under the porch.

I'll just put my watch in my pocket. Now, I've looked everywhere– except in the shed.

Wow! I'm too dressed up to work in the garden now. Kitten, what are you doing?